This Time Of Our Lives

This Time Of Our Lives

living through the menopause

poems by

Maggie Simmonds

Date of Publication:
September 1999

Published by:
Red Priors Print
Lower End, Priors Hardwick
CV47 7SP

Printed by:
ProPrint
Riverside Cottage
Great North Road
Stibbington
Peterborough PE8 6LR

ISBN: 0 9537084 0 3

These verses are dedicated to the most influential woman in my life, my beloved Mum, the late Dorothy Redfern, née Simmonds.

For some of us this time will pass
Uneventfully
As a blade of grass
Stands firm in a whispering wind.

For others it will be a time
When life will seem devoid of rhyme
Tranquillity or reason.

Just as each season
Passes into the next
We can expect and know
We will come through.

Whatever form our 'pause may take
We can stand firm, we need not break
If we are patient with ourselves
And tell the world 'hold on
Give me time'
As we become
Women of Wisdom.

Acknowledgements

My thanks to the many people who have been with me on my journey - family, friends, colleagues, teachers and especially those who live with me.

CONTENTS:

Section 1   *The Menopause Experience*

Section 2   *Other Happenings*

Section 3   *Taking Care of Ourselves*

The Menopause Experience

Menopause Poem

This is ridiculous!
A few moments ago I was down, in the depths.
Now my spirit is high, optimistic, I have plans
To publish poems,
To teach
To empower others.
I am cool, I am calm.
Just then I was hot, claustrophobic.
My body is a roller coaster.
From the heights to the depths
I plunge
Then slowly crawl out.
Hands are cold now, so are feet.
Grab that sweater, turn up the heat.
Exhaustion and despair
Interspersed with exhilaration:
Memory losses, dizzy spells.
And the part that keeps me going:
That wonderful taste,
From time to time,
Of what must surely be
Post-Menopausal Zest.

Drained

Limbs won't move, head is tingly,
Thoughts come slowly, won't be hurried.
Shoulders heavy, craving rest.
Lying down gives comfort, respite
Standing up's like climbing mountains.
Every movement slow and laboured
Body weight feels dull and languid
As if it's lead dragging through my veins

Women in Transition

Jan enjoys her hot flushes
They keep her warm
In winter.
She doesn't like forgetting things -
The name, place or event
She can't remember
In the middle
Of a conversation.

Gill decided when one day
A pupil said, 'Oh Miss, you're red'
That HRT was the way.
For her it was okay.

Joy is determined that hot flushes or no,
On that route she won't go
And uses agnus castus
To try to cool the glow.

Maggie fears the panic
When, while she's out
Her confidence deserts her
And she's riddled through with doubt.

Paula's bed is regularly soaked
With intense night sweats
Pamela fears her constant tears
Will never ever end.

Judith, lucky Judith
No symptoms ever had,
Her periods stopped
And that was that.
Doesn't it make you mad,
To see what some endure?

One thing's for sure -
We're all unique,
Our signs and symptoms vary,
The hardest bit's the 'wait and see'
Not knowing if it's over
When all seems calm and clear again.
Or will there be
Another deep depression
Before our wise woman in the wings
Can take centre stage?

Suffocating

We sat in her private practice
Which fitted her so well:
Clear, bright, calm and welcoming.
So different from the perched-on chairs
We had used in the surgery,
Fitting in wherever was free.
Those rooms which reflected the arrogance
And fitted-into-drawers-individuals
Whose territories they were
And we were borrowing.
Suffocating - she described my condition
Then.
When we had met and shared
Credentials,
Agreed to work together
To set out to make some sense of the
Anguish I was experiencing.
Suffocating. Yes, I had been there
In that barrenness where
Energy, vivacity, initiative and enthusiasm
Had long been used up, drained and sucked from me.

Into the Light

The patch ahead is radiant with light.
The sun is shining down into this vacuum in front of me.
I can go forward into it, surrounded by warmth
And brightness
And leave the dark behind.

Unbidden Guest

There's nothing specific to worry about today
And yet it's there,
That feeling inside
Which borders on panic.

I'm breathing deeply, that helps.
I can think better now.

It just arrives sometimes, a darkness within,
No notice, no greeting 'I'm here because . . . '
And if I don't work hard to stop it
It takes over.

My chest thumps,
The tingles start at the back of my head,
Stomach sick and in turmoil,
Fear - of something unknown
Engulfs me.

This 'guest' without a name
Arrives unannounced, unbidden.

Contrasts

Vivid hose-reel green and brown-yellow strawey grass
Rain-dropped mauve primulas wobbling on their stems
Browning yellow roses, bowed by water weight
Shining raindrops hanging from the climbing frame.
The blackbird on the telephone wires chatter
Is exercising it totally.
It jerks in time.

Inside the glass
All is fawn, dull and stale.

This Time of My Life

This time of my life has been one of anguish,
Of terror and hopelessness, fear and despair.
With patches of light and hope in-between-times
Looking forward to the freedom I seek when it ends.

Each changing phase and repeated pattern,
Always the questions,
Is it over?
Am I free?
Then hopes dashed by realisation
That no, I'm not there yet.
I'm still on the treadmill of
Hormonal chaos,
Emotional pain.

This time of my life seems to bring to the surface
So many sad memories, the losses, the lacks,
The burdens, the hang-ups, the ways it might have been
Emerge from the cellar - all the darknesses I've seen.

Today I've decided to give up the yearning,
The longing, the waiting for this phase to end.

While I'm doing all that, I'm wasting the chances
For learning and being that every day brings.

So however long it runs for
I'll go with it freely
Accepting the hiccups,
The ebb and the flow.
I'll swim through the clouds
I'll dance in the rainbows
And confirm to myself what I already know.

A Woman

I am a woman who is wise but does not always know
That this is so.
I am a woman who can love and give and hope and be
But this isn't always clear to me.
I am a woman who is young and old at once
Who can teach and learn - and be a dunce.
I am a woman who is possessed with what really matters
And sometimes I don't know anything at all.
Just that being can be hard, can be good, can be cruel.
And I go on being
Me.

Taking Stock

Fifty-two next week
And I'm still here
In this so-called 'no-man's-land'

No, that's not quite true,
It is less barren, much less barren
Than it was before.
I have moved and
It has changed, mellowed.
The landscape is kinder now,
I know I can get through.
The path is softer
The steep narrow chasms have become rounded hills.

My body is stronger, my mind more clear,
My wisdom and knowledge are firmer
More sure.
Already I can look back, though it's tentative yet,
See where I was earlier
And know
That the me of now is different from before.

Fifty-two next week and getting there.

Right Now

Where I am is perfect
For what I need right now.
Energy may be high or low
And while I may not know the reason
And may feel
I want to be elsewhere and doing more
Of what makes my heart sing,
Where I am is perfect - for now.

Recovery

My body is healing
Slowly recovering
From the months and the years
Of keeping going
And pushing against itself to go on.

My mind is healing,
Gradually clearing
To be open to life
No longer chained to that rut.

My spirit is healing
Slowly rising,
Like a timid moon
It's rising, rising, gradually rising.

My being is healing
Becoming whole
Finding itself again
In laughter and stillness
And me.

Where?

Yet again I'm losing things
First the key, now my favourite ring.
Last week it was my briefcase,
Yesterday my watch.
I put them down and just then I know
Exactly where they are.
But later when I come to look
I've no idea where I put
The thing I'm looking for.

People Like You

She exudes vitality
Speaks with authority
Contributes ideas,
Experience
Facts.
She is in command
Of her life,
Of her job.
She's okay.

As we sit at the table
Enjoying our soup
She tells me the other side
Of her experience now.

Panic, despair, hot flushes
And fear.
That dark unbidden fear
Which shakes the foundation of our being
Questions our judgement, our control, our experience
Erodes our memory,
Challenges our sanity
Engulfs us in tears
Helter-skelters us between depression and mania
And leaves us exhausted.

No inkling of timing,
How long we will be on this stage of our journey
Buffeting between tempest, half-drowned becalmment
And normality.

Lines on the Road from Kilmun

When we first met
You seemed remote
Not coldly distant but so accomplished,
So articulate, so very skilled.

When we met elsewhere
I saw your sadness
Your vulnerability,
The tests you faced.
We found some common bonds
And formed a link
Across the distance between our lives.

And so we meet, your lochside home
Finding so much we can compare
Now in this time of our maturing
As women of wisdom
So much to share.

Lonely Journey

We are travelling an unknown road.
Not untravelled, just unknown because we are all
Different.
Our ancestresses have gone before.
They suffered too.
Some were entombed
In hospitals or took their lives because
They could endure no more
These symptoms of the changes
Our bodies battle through.

Dear Sister

As I tied up the Celebration Rose you gave me
Its golden-cream perfection
Reminded me
That we,
Though so different,
Share that strong maternal link
And I knew I needed to tell you.

You are now the age that I was when it started.
The headaches and panic,
The tears and creeping depression.
This is the time before blood tests can show
And we need to know
It has begun.
It's called 'peri'
Prior to the 'pause
Its effects can be very extreme.
While our doctors may tell us
We aren't there yet,
We need to realise it has begun.

You're not going mad.
Nor are you alone.

For those it challenges this time of our lives
Can be one of confusion
Of fear for our minds.
Our bodies seem to leave us
In limbo or worse.
How was it we called
What came earlier 'the curse'?

This may rock our foundations, leave us weary,
Feeling scared.
It seems endless, takes us deeper
To depths so low
We did not know existed.
And yet through it we grow,
Recognise our wisdom,
Reach the core
Of who we are
And know ourselves.

Source of Information

Did you tell me that?
I'm sorry, I forgot.
There seems to be a blank spot
In my memory just there.

Yes, as you tell me more
It seems familiar.

Are you sure
I didn't read it in a book
Or on a sign somewhere?
I don't remember hearing it
From you.

It's Wonderful to Know

Yes, it's wonderful to know I know it all!

Do please read on.
This is not the arrogant statement it may seem.

It is wonderful to know that all I need
Is here inside me
Waiting to be seen, heard, recognised,
Remembered -
After so long of looking outside.

Thanks to my teachers, counsellors, friends
Who helped me find the key,
I now recognise it's all here in me
Waiting to be found.

Nearest and Dearest

A mum who snaps,
A wife in tears,
My family ask
'For how many years
Must we put up with this?'

Yes, they've been used
To PMT
The ups and downs of living with me.
This seems like a permanent crescendo
Of irritability and tiredness.
Rare smile in the gloom.

Putting the Pieces Together

It's as if my whole existence
Is encapsulated
In this time.
By turns childlike and a crone
Innocent and wise.
My eyes
More blurred, seeing less clearly,
My inward vision
And intuition
Seeing more.

I remember
Relive the pains
Shed some of the tears
Kept in my barrel of sadness
For years.

And I move through and on
To new levels of understanding
And feeling and thinking.

And the jigsaw is nearer to completion.

Moving On

I do not remember cycling down the hill today.

And yet for years
My fears
Kept the brakes full on
My hands gripping, my mind racing
As I hung on down that hill.

I do not remember coming down the hill today.

Life's Unpredictabilities

'Wait a minute please,
Just a mo',
Yes, of course I'd like to go.'
(Please be patient,
Can't you see
Life is playing tricks on me.
Can't find my specs
And, recently,
I'm helpless without them).
'Yes, I'm ready, just need my bag
And a coat.' 'No, it's not a joke,
I know it's hot today
But while we're on the way
I may well bake and also soak
In perspiration two minutes later.'

'Yes, I'm okay really,
Still the same me you've always known
It's just that while my hormones
Are constantly on the move
I'm never quite sure
What will happen next.'

Other Happenings

As

I take stock of the weariness
Which has brought me to this point
Of change.

The old is finished.

I turn out the papers
And neatly arrange the mementoes.

The new is strange
After so long without change
And·what I really want

Is just to stand still

Aquarobics with Iris

'Is anybody pregnant?'
'Any bad backs?'
The music starts and Iris
Demonstrates the moves.
'Enjoy yourself' is the message
As we sway and stretch,
Gently at first
Then jog, jump and clap
Through a medley of tunes and tempos.
She swings in time, we follow.
We exercise, laugh and enjoy
The movement, the water (when it's not too cold)
And the company.
Queen of the poolside she encourages,
Challenges and applauds our efforts
And makes it fun.

Possible Dream

I did it,
It happened,
I fulfilled my 'impossible dream'.
What I thought could never be,
Really was
Done by me.
And now I know
Nothing's impossible.
If you really do believe you can do it,
You can.

For Anne on a Special Birthday

Friendship is a sheltering tree,
A listening ear
A welcoming smile.

Friendship is a hug, a touch,
Being there when times are sad,
Encouraging all along the way
Sharing laughter, fun, success.

Picking up where we left off
Our lifetime conversation.

For all of this and so much more,
Thank you.

'Lucy'

I loved you so dearly
It was as if
The umbilical cord had not been cut.

A thread linked me to you
Invisible,
Indiscernible.
It made our partings
Heart deep,
Kept me beside you
So that I needed to go far away and
Test its elasticity.

The thread was endless.
Our closeness did not dissipate with distance.

Now you are that skylark winging,
Singing
In the February early spring.
As I continue on my journey,
My separate self, .
I love you just as dearly.

Her Daughter

Your blue eyes were shaded with grey today
I saw the liveliness in your smile
Temporarily dimmed.
The sadness had returned.

She is not gone
But is here in each one of us,
A look, a phrase, a thoughtful act.
The kindness you show to others
You learnt from her.

Can you confront your anger,
Let it rage,
Till you are free
To be
Yourself - a colourful kaleidoscope
Of talent and feeling.
Some of these colours were gifts from her.

Feel her mantle around you,
Hear her laugh in the sounds of birds.
See her smile in the face of flowers
And know she, too, is free.

Yesterday Would Have Been Your Birthday

Yesterday would have been your birthday.
It still was I suppose.
I missed being able to see you
To visit you with gifts and love.

You visited me last night in dream
And you had moved.
You were no longer in the family home of childhood
From where you left us,
The place of garden, orchard, pump and lamplight
Of gentle morning sun and evening thunder:
But in a timeless place of convenience,
Calm and emotionless.

Perhaps I, too, can move on?

I Think of it Always Being Sunny Here

Each month we brought our lives
And shared some part of growth or grief
Our feelings, hopes and expectations.
We wept, explored, kept silence.
We challenged sometimes, raged a little.
Supported by that mutual love
We opened doors long closed,
And dusted boxes kept on shelves
Opened them a chink
Or put them back.

Some skills grew strong
Some proved elusive.
We were the recipients
While becoming the givers.
We knew the pain, saw change,
In ourselves and others
The reality and metaphorically:
Just as we untied the human knot
With laughter, contortions and good-humoured suggestion.
We practised and played, we read and reacted
Through to that final day of self-validation.

Some days it rained
The sun often did shine.
The central heating's time-table
Lacked congruence with ours.

The thread that did not break:
The warmth of women for women.

Conversation

'Where do you start to write a poem
Or create a song?'

'Where do you start to paint a picture?'

An idea,
A response to an emotion.
Something else, too,
An energy which appears, bubbles up,
Is somehow there, for that moment.

Coming from where?
A hand guiding?
A voice speaking?

A flow of creativity
From within
Which finds expression
Sometimes easily,
At others laboured
As it makes its way
Through hand to paper
And is lovingly born.

The painting is part mystical
While capturing
Things which are real,
Colourful and feeling.

It hangs in the hall, elegantly framed.

We Won The Lottery

We won the lottery!
Not personally, we aren't millionaires or anything.
It's the organisation that's won.
You remember, when we filled in that long form.
It took hours, seemed like days,
All that pencil-chewing
And re-phrasing words.
We knew what we wanted to do
But putting it down on paper wasn't easy.
Anyway we finished it, posted it off and sat back to hope.

Then that assessor came, do you remember?
He sounded rather stiff and starchy on the 'phone.
We were a bit nervous.
He was impressed though,
Said he could feel the energy of our ideas
And the way we worked together.
That's what cracked it I think.
(He did like the biscuits, too, they were the special ones -
From the health food shop).

So now we know, after all those weeks of waiting to see.
We've done it.
We can do the work we planned and dreamed of.

We won the lottery.

Square Peg

I came here because
I thought it was my place
I came here because
I liked the idea.

I came here without asking the questions
I should have.
I thought it was right.
I thought it was clear.

I've been here,
I've learnt.
I know it's not my place.

Tomorrow, I'm going to somewhere that's me.

International Women's Day Celebration

Purple for dignity
White for purity
Green for hope.

These colours and symbols
Salute and celebrate
The splendour of womankind
Active here.

A meeting of minds,
Of faces,
Of interests,
Discussing concerns,
Hopes and fears.

Women together
Sharing,
Learning,
Caring,
Planning,
Being themselves.

Our challenges are different
Our demands have moved on.
The women before us
Their battle won,
To
Give
Women the
Vote

Empty Nest

'Hello?'
'No, I'm sorry,
He isn't here.
He went up to University
Yesterday.'

Away.
Flown the nest.
'Yes, I'm doing my best.'

But it seems very odd.
Quiet.
Empty.

Wrong Number

He doesn't live here any more.
If you just hold the line
I'll find the address
And give you his number.

Yes, we're still in touch.
Good friends in fact.
That helps the children too.
They were rather afraid
When we went separate ways
They'd be the centre of a tennis match.

Yes thank you,
I'm fine.
After those months of hell
I'm doing very well.
I'm healthy, I'm free.
At last life's a breeze -
Only have myself to please.
My career's on the up
Sorry, I must hang up,
A friend's just come to collect me.

Brothers' Reunion

'This is a bit different from
Two hundred and six Sish Lane,
Gordon,' he said
As he sat at the head of the dining table
In his Scottish riverside home.
They sipped wine
And remembered
Digging holes for lead soldiers,
Throwing shovels of earth for ammunition.
They chuckled, chortled and laughed uproariously
As they talked of the people,
Their own tricks and activities.
Remembering the plentiful fun -
No mention of gaps or sorrows,
Happy at the distance
Between then and now.

The Lone Rangers

The door opens, a welcoming smile,
'The kettle's on.'
One comes early, one dashes in,
The absent one is missed.

For this hour
We unload our burdens,
Let slip the mask of superwoman,
Tear off the tag 'guilty because woman'
And we listen, open our hearts,
Share and encourage.
Laugh and cry
In this peace of togetherness.

The door opens,
A warm farewell.
'Take care.'
'See you next time.'

On Your Retirement

The end of an era?
A bright new beginning!
The time to be you,
To do as you will
At your pace and choice.
No timetables,
'Orders'
Or even instructions.
The chance for reflection, development,
Space.
Your talents can flow,
Your creativity free
To make your own world
As you want it to be.

Summer Standstill

Sitting on the beach with a broken pen
Wanting to express the ease I feel,
Several days away from
The dis-easing world of work.

All is calm, sea, sky and me.
Almost becalmed by this total standstill.
People sitting, lying, lazing
And forgetting
The realities of home-life; rush-hours, mortgage,
Kept at a distance by
The long outbreath of the withdrawing sea.

Envy rises in me as I hear
'You're here for six weeks.'
'We live here.'
And I think how much progress my healing body
Would make if this time was unlimited.

But then I know that there are things to do
I want to do.
And they are not all in
This place of calm.

Philosophy

God the father?
Not for me.
I do not want a god
Who is austere
And tells me I should do things
Because he says so.

My god is warm, all-embracing
Universal.
Not 'he'
Not strict, judgmental or male
Just being and free.
We're all part of this life force
Which allows and encourages,
Supports and protects us.

We're all one, all god

People Place

I have walked this street for sixteen years
Most weekday mornings,
Many weeks of the year
Towards this building.

It started as two ups and downs,
Became a sweet shop, windows barred
Then changed to offices.
We call it house, though not a home now
It is a haven for some.
A place to talk and share and be
What you know you have potential to.
A community place, small and warm
In spirit, if not temperature.
It's chilly in winter
Offers coolth in summer heat.
Its walls could tell of all who've come
To help, support or who aspire
To make some change to the lives of those
Who pass through
Here.

Taking Care of Ourselves

The poems Meditation and Relaxation can be used for relaxation if you read them slowly onto a tape and play them with your eyes closed sitting in a comfortable position, spine erect.

Meditation

Take yourself gently by the hand
Just sit there and be for a while.
Nothing to fear
Nothing to do.
Listen to your breath.
Look inside and see You.

Take a deep breath and
Slowly let it go
As you ponder with wonder
The beauty of your being.

Feel your spine erect
Strong, exquisite,
Creation of nature
Intricacy of bone.
Feel your limbs
Now still,
Which move and guide you
With limitless grace.
Your beating heart,
Ever pumping,
Giving strength all around
This temple of womankind.

And your mind
Which is boundless
With possibilities to be and to do.

Look to your breath again
And enjoy
The inward rising
The slow release.

Appreciate your wholeness,
Your oneness,
The inner peace
You give yourself
When you recognise
The wonderful being that you are.

Sit quietly with this truth.

Lie or sit down ensuring that you are comfortable. Take a deep breath and let it out with a sigh.

Relaxation

This time is for you
To relax and let go,
To tune in to yourself
And to get to know
The real you
Inside the face you put on
To show the world outside.
Your breath is your way in to the quietness and calm.

Now slowly breathe in, a big life-giving breath -
Balm
To your weary being.

Feel your toes and feet relaxing.
Breathe in again and, slowly breathing out,
Feel your legs, knees and thighs
Sinking into the floor or the chair
Where you now
Feel supported,
Feel relaxed
As your breath ebbs and flows.

Breathing in again and then letting go,
Feel your buttocks, your waist,
Your beautiful back which you know
Works so hard to keep you upright,
Surrendering to a pace of tranquillity.

Take a breath down to your stomach
And as it leaves
Feel the tension you are holding there evaporate -
The knots and ruckles smoothing out
As you sink a little further into calm.

Take a breath and as you sigh it out
Your shoulders and chest
Feel loose, feel free
As you blow away the stress.

Now your arms are letting go,
All the way down
From your shoulders to your finger tips.
As your breath caresses
Each part, each joint.
You know you are relaxing,
Letting go of any strain.

Feel your neck and your head,
Release your jaw, soften your eyes
Let any frown disappear.
Feel your face
Is the face of a child - open and smooth.
Welcome it with love.

From your feet to the top of your head
You are soft and relaxed.
Your breath is leading and supporting you
Spreading calmness
Bringing true
Relaxation

The Goddess - a Song

See the goddess before you
See the goddess before you.
What colour is her hair?
What colour are her eyes?
See the goddess before you
See the goddess before you.

That goddess is inside you
That goddess is inside you
Feel her strength and know her wisdom
Move her dance and be her rhythm.
That goddess is inside you,
That goddess is inside you,

She is you.
She is you.

Time Out

Just stop,
Stand still.
Take a breath
And let it go.
You don't have to do all the chores
Now you know.
There's always tomorrow,
Next week,
Next Spring.
Don't expect yourself
To do everything.

Take a really deep breath,
Sigh it out,
Let it go.
Before you sit down
Turn the music to low.
Put your feet up,
Lie back,
Take some time for yourself.
Think 'this is for me',
Relaxing,
Just being
And feeling free.

Affirmation

I am strong
I feel my power
I speak my truth
I sing my song.